Heads Up!
Puzzles For Sports Brains

BY BRAD HERZOG

Joel Abacherli

A *Sports Illustrated For Kids* Book

Bantam Books

NEW YORK • TORONTO • LONDON • SYDNEY • AUCKLAND

Heads Up: Puzzles for Sports Brains by Brad Herzog

A Bantam Book/March 1994

SPORTS ILLUSTRATED FOR KIDS and **KIDS** are registered trademarks of
Time Inc.
SPORTS ILLUSTRATED FOR KIDS BOOKS are published in cooperation
with Bantam Doubleday Dell Publishing Group, Inc. under license from Time
Inc.

Cover and interior design by Miriam Dustin

ISBN 0-553-48160-6

Published simultaneously in the United States and Canada

Bantam books are published by Bantam Books, a division of Bantam Doubleday
Dell Publishing Group, Inc. Its trademark, consisting of the words "Bantam
Books" and the portrayal of a rooster, is Registered in the U.S. Patent and
Trademark Office and in other countries. Marca Registrada. Bantam Books,
1540 Broadway, New York, NY 10036

Printed in the United States of America

CWO 0 9 8 7 6 5 4 3 2 1

TAKE THE CHALLENGE!

A team of sports experts wrote these puzzles. The puzzles are fun, they're challenging, and some of them even have trick plays! If you're in these experts' league, tackling these puzzles will prove it. Sign up here, then turn the page. The tournament of games is about to begin!

TWO-SPORT QUIZ

Some words mean one thing in one sport, but have a different meaning in another sport. For example, in football, a *field goal* means kicking the ball through the goalposts, but, in basketball, a *field goal* is another name for scoring a basket. Can you figure out the word with two meanings in each of the rhyming verses below? Fill in the words and then write the shaded letters in order in the spaces at the end of the puzzle to find the name of a famous two-sport star!

This term is used in auto racing,
and you do it carefully to stay alive.
But in golf when you step up to the tee,
you use your biggest club to _____.   ▨ __ __ __ __

You use your hands to do this
in the sport played by Shaquille O'Neal.
But Rickey Henderson uses his feet
when he wants to _steal_.   __ __ ▨ __ __

This word means "toss" in two sports.
Can you figure out which is which?
In horseshoes you throw the shoes,
but in baseball you throw a _____.   __ ▨ __ __ __

You take one of these to score a basket
(Charles Barkley takes a lot).
But a metal ball thrown in field events
is also called a _____.   __ __ ▨ __

In wrestling, if you make this move,
you automatically win.
But in bowling, if you bowl a nine,
that means you've left one _pin_.   __ __ ▨

4

In hoops, this word goes with "dunk,"
and sometimes it's called a "jam."
In baseball, when there are three men on,
a homer is a grand _Slam_ .   ☐ __ __ __

A race car driver sees a checkered one
when the race is "in the bag."
But a football referee's is yellow.
On a penalty, he throws a _Flag_ .   __ __ ☐ __

In a football game, unless you've passed,
this is what you've done.
But when you cross the plate in baseball
you've scored your team a _____ .   __ __ ☐

He's a blocker on a football team,
a lineman who works hard.
But Michael Jordan also plays
the position called a _____ .   __ __ __ __ ☐

Some people like to walk through woods,
just like some ride a bike.
But a quarterback also says this word
when he calls, "Ready, set, _Hike_ !"   __ __ __ ☐

This term can mean a perfect frame
if bowling is what you like.
Or it could mean a swing and miss
and an umpire saying, "_Strike_ !"   __ __ ☐ __ __

You can throw a runner out in baseball
with one flick of the wrist.
But a great pass that leads to a hoop
in basketball is called an _____ .   __ ☐ __ __ __ __

TWO-SPORT STAR:

__ __ __ __ __ __   __ __ __ __ __ __

5

WORD SPIRAL

A spiral is the best way to throw a football, but it is also a fun way to solve a puzzle. Fill in the answers in the grid on the next page in a clockwise direction (↷). Each word ends at the space where you see the next number. The last letter of each word will be the first letter of the next word. Answers 1 and 2 have been filled in to show you how it works. Some answers will have to be written in backward. When the puzzle is done, you will see a bonus nine-letter word down the shaded column on the grid!

1. To hit a ball, a batter has to **SWING**.
2. A field goal is good if it goes through the middle of the **GOALPOST**.
3. A golfer sometimes places the golf ball on top of a _____.
4. To score a touchdown, you must reach the _____.
5. If a hockey team takes out the goalie, that means it leaves an _____ net.
6. The best pitcher in each league wins the Cy _____ Award.
7. What all baseball fielders wear
8. The best athletes in basketball are chosen to play in the All-_____ Game.
9. Los Angeles has two football teams: the Rams and the _____.
10. The players on a team who don't start are often called the second _____.
11. In football, the offense tries to _____ yardage.
12. New Jersey's basketball team

13. How Spud Webb feels when standing next to Patrick Ewing.
14. What you call a member of your team
15. The most famous daredevil: _____ Knievel
16. The opposite of a win is a _____.
17. A short word for substitute
18. What the batter does on a squeeze play
19. Another word for throw (rhymes with boss)
20. Beach volleyball is played in the _____.

¹S	W	I	N	²G	O	A	L	P
	8			9				O
		14						S
		18			19			³T
							10	
7	13	17		20		15		4
				16				
		12			11			
	6				5			

SECRET WORD:

___ ___ ___ ___ ___ ___ ___ ___ ___

7

DOUBLE JEOPARDY #1

Hit a double when you solve this puzzle! Below are 7 athletes' names but they're all mixed up! Unscramble them in the spaces on the right (**hint**: the symbol is their sport) Then write the letters from the shaded boxes in order in the secret name spaces below to spell out an NFL team.

1. **TAMT SLIMWALI** ___ ___ ___ ___ ___
___ ___ ___ ___ ___ ___ ___

2. **YARLR SNOJHON** ___ ___ ___ ___ ___
___ ___ ___ ___ ___ ___

3. **NIBRO VENUART** ___ ___ ___ ___ ___
___ ___ ___ ___ ___ ___

4. **FEFITS FARG** ___ ___ ___ ___ ___
___ ___ ___ ___

5. **LARK NAMELO** ___ ___ ___ ___
___ ___ ___ ___ ___

6. **STETCOI PINPEP** ___ ___ ___ ___ ___ ___
___ ___ ___ ___ ___

7. **GREOR MELSNEC** ___ ___ ___ ___ ___
___ ___ ___ ___ ___ ___

SECRET NAME: ___ ___ ___ ___ ___ ___ ___ ___
___ ___ ___ ___ ___ ___

8

SPORTS SCATTERGRAM

Betty opened her closet and look what came spilling out!
Every piece of equipment below but one is shown
twice. Can you find the one piece of equipment that just
appears once on this page?

9

SAME NAME GAME

Some top athletes share the same first name, such as football player Eric Dickerson and baseball player Eric Davis. On this page is a list of 16 first names, and on the next are 16 sets of last names. The athletes in each group of last names share the same first name. Can you match the first names below with the last names on the right? We've done the first for you. (**Hint**: we've put a picture of the sport the athlete plays next to their last name.)

~~Joe~~	~~John~~	~~Terry~~	~~Barry~~
~~Chris~~	~~Andre~~	~~Jack~~	~~Dennis~~
~~Jim~~	~~Fred~~	~~Tom~~	~~Tim~~
~~Michael~~	~~Paul~~	~~Steve~~	~~Charles~~

WRITE IN THE FIRST NAMES HERE:

1. **MICHAEL**
2. Andre
3. Chris
4. Terry
5. John
6. Charles
7. Barry
8. Jim
9. Steve
10. Tom
11. Dennis
12. Jack
13. Joe
14. Tim
15. Paul
16. Fred

10

1. Chang , Irvin , Jordan

2. Dawson , Agassi , Reed

3. Mullin , Doleman , Chelios , Bosio

4. Pendleton , Porter

5. Elway , Kruk , Stockton , McEnroe

6. Barkley , Oakley , Nagy

7. Sanders , Foster , Larkin , Bonds

8. Courier , Abbott , Harbaugh

9. Young , Avery , Yzerman

10. Glavine , Kite , Chambers

11. Eckersley , Rodman

12. McDowell , Morris , Nicklaus

13. Carter , Montana , Dumars

14. Hardaway , Raines

15. Coffey , Molitor

16. McGriff , Couples

GRIDIRON CROSSWORD

Tackle this crossword and test your knowledge of football!

ACROSS

1. A defensive player tries to _____ the man with the ball.
3. It's not whether you win or lose, but how you _____ the game.
6. This play is worth two points.
8. These people call heads or tails in the pregame coin flip.
10. The plays leading up to a touchdown make up the touchdown _____.
11. Lawrence Taylor's nickname
12. The biggest game of the NFL season is the Super _____.
14. To score a touchdown, you must cross the _____.
16. John Elway's initials
17. After a touchdown, the kicker tries for the _____ point.
19. To call a penalty, a referee throws a yellow _____.
20. Most NFL games are played on this day

DOWN

1. This play is worth six points.
2. Blocking illegally from behind
3. The offense has a choice on every play: run or _____.
4. The Green _____ Packers
5. A backwards or sideways pass is called a _____.
7. If a player loses the ball, it is called a _____.
9. The abbreviation for National Football League
13. If you don't win or tie, you _____.

15. An abbreviation for interception
17. You score a touchdown by reaching the _____ zone with the ball.
18. The abbreviation of the American Football Conference

BOWLING FOR LETTERS

The following are eight scrambled words or phrases, each in the shape of a set of bowling pins. Each word or phrase has 10 letters and each counts as one frame in a bowling game. Can you find the 10-letter word in each group? If not, what's the largest word you can find? Multiply the number of letters in the largest word you come up with by three, and that will be your score for the frame.

For example, in the first frame you can find a 10-letter word — GYMNASTICS. That gives you 30 (10 letters **x** 3) points. But if the largest word you found was a five-letter word — STING, for example — you would get 15 (5 x 3) points. Remember, some of the scrambles are two word phrases (such as second base). All of the 10-letter words are familiar sports terms. Now have fun bowling for letters!

```
            C I M Y
1st FRAME:  G A N
              T S      word: Gymnastics  points: 30
              S
```

```
            B K S T
2nd FRAME:  E L L
              B A      word: _____  points: _____
              A
```

```
            N E L I
3rd FRAME:  B E R
              C K      word: _____  points: _____
              A
```

4th FRAME:

```
    G L F C
    O U S
    R E
    O
```
word: _____ points: _____

5th FRAME:

```
    V E B A
    O L L
    L Y
    L
```
word: _____ points: _____

6th FRAME:

```
    G L A O
    T E R
    N D
    E
```
word: _____ points: _____

7th FRAME:

```
    D U B L
    E A P
    L Y
    O
```
word: _____ points: _____

8th FRAME:

```
    A C K B
    K S T
    R E
    O
```
word: _____ points: _____

TOTAL SCORE:

___ + ___ + ___ + ___ + ___ + ___ + ___ + ___

= _____ POINTS

15

A, B, SIERRA

Can you match each of the 15 athletes with the letter that can be heard in his or her **last** name? On the left is a list of 15 letters. On the right is a list of 15 athletes. Say each athlete's **last** name out loud. The sound of a particular letter of the alphabet can be heard in each player's name. For example, if you say, "Ruben Sierra" out loud, you can hear the letter " C " in "Sierra." If you say, " Monica Seles," you can hear the letter " L " in "Seles." Each athlete is matched with just one letter, so if you hear two letters in a name, make sure you pick the right one.

LETTERS

A B C D

G J L M

O T U V

X Y Z

ATHLETES

_____ JOHN ELWAY

_____ OZZIE SMITH

_____ PATRICK EWING

_____ TIM HARDAWAY

_____ EMMITT SMITH

_____ MARK MCGWIRE

_____ REGGIE WHITE

_____ DAVEY ALLISON

_____ DEE BROWN

_____ JAY SCHROEDER

_____ JENNIFER CAPRIATI

_____ ANDRE AGASSI

_____ CLYDE DREXLER

_____ KIRBY PUCKETT

_____ DAN MARINO

TWO TIMES TWO

Have twice the fun with these athletes who have two double-letter combinations in their names. For example, in football player William Perry's name, you can see an " LL " and an " RR." In baseball player Jeff Bagwell's name there's an " FF " and an " LL ." Fit the double-letters from the box on the right into the athletes' names. Then look at the numbers under some of the letters. Put each "numbered" letter in the correct numbered space at the bottom of the page, and spell out the name of the NBA player who once averaged a "triple double" (at least 10 points, 10 rebounds, and 10 assists per game) over an entire NBA season!

WA _ _ E N M _ _ N
     6   1 7

BRE _ _ HU _ _

E _ _ I _ _ SMITH
9   12

BO _ _ Y BONI _ _ A
    8   13   4

SCO _ _ IE PI _ _ EN
2   11

RANDA _ _ CU _ _ INGHAM
        3   14

DA _ _ YL STRAWBE _ _ Y
  5   10

TT	LL	RR
MM	TT	RR
LL	NN	TT
PP	RR	BB
LL	OO	

___ ___ ___ ___ ___
1   2   3   4   5

___ ___ ___ ___ ___ ___ ___ ___ ___
6   7   8   9 10 11 12 13 14

17

FOOTBALL FILL-IN

We have kicked off this puzzle for you by writing FORTY NINERS in its proper space in the grid on the next page. Can you finish the fill-in, using the list of the 27 NFL team names on this page? The teams are divided up by the number of letters in each team name. Cross out the teams as you go along. Ready, set, hike!

4 LETTERS
Jets
Rams

7 LETTERS
Bengals
Broncos
Cowboys
Falcons
Packers
Raiders
Vikings

5 LETTERS
Bears
Bills
Colts
Lions

8 LETTERS
Chargers
Dolphins
Patriots
Redskins
Seahawks
Steelers

6 LETTERS
Browns
Chiefs
Eagles
Giants
Oilers
Saints

9 LETTERS
Cardinals

10 LETTERS
Buccaneers

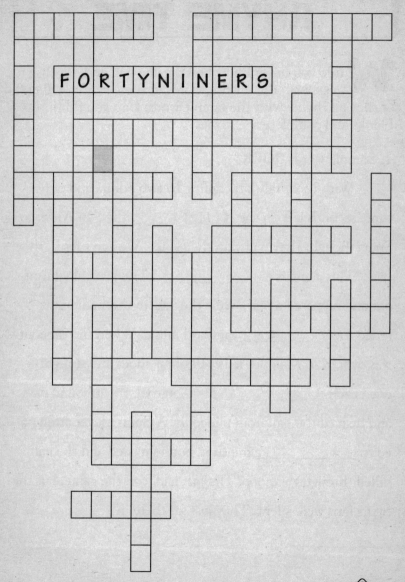

FORTYNINERS

RHYME TIME

While you never know how a game will end, it's easy to guess how the missing words in these stories will end —they all rhyme with the sample word! Can you fill in the blanks and complete the stories?

1. Sample word: **DOCK**

With the Utah Jazz trailing by two points and only three seconds left on the _clock_, the San Antonio Spurs thought they had won the game. "We can't lose," they said. "This game is a _____." The Jazz called time-out and prepared a play, while the fans in the stadium listened to _Rock_ and roll music. When the timeout was over, Karl Malone tied each of his shoes and straightened each _____. He then took the inbound pass and heaved the ball from midcourt. A Spurs player attempted to _____ the shot, but he missed and the ball sailed through the hoop. The Jazz had won the game, but the Spurs fans were silent. They just sat there in

_____.

2. Sample word: **BUN**

     The _____ was setting on the football field and the _____ was about to sound, signaling the end of the game. The Detroit Lions had the ball on their own 30-yard line. They trailed the Green Bay Packers by five points, and there were only four seconds left to play. But the Lions' coach knew the game wasn't quite ____done____ yet. There was time for one more play, and he had to make a decision: pass or _____? He decided to give the ball to Barry Sanders, who broke six tackles and sped 70 yards for a touchdown. "That was _____!" Barry said after the game. "Especially because we _____."

THE SUM-MER GAME

Did you know that homerun hitters Hank Aaron, Reggie Jackson, and Willie McCovey all wore the same uniform number? To find out that number, complete this puzzle. Read the clue and put the correct number — 1 through 12 — in the correct space, and keep adding or subtracting, whichever the puzzle tells you to do. At the end, you'll have the sluggers' favorite number.

Number of players on the offense of a football team   11

                                                    PLUS +

Number of years between each Summer Olympics   _____

                                                    MINUS –

Number of rings in the Olympic flag   6

                                                    PLUS +

Number of runs scored on two grand slams   6

                                                    PLUS +

Number of points for a safety in football   2

                                                    PLUS +

Number of minutes in a quarter in an NBA game   10

                                                    PLUS +

Number of fielders on a baseball field   _____

                                                    PLUS +

Number of points for a touchdown   _____

                                                    MINUS –

Number of strikes in baseball when you're out   _____

THE MAGIC NUMBER IS _____

ON THE MARK

Make <u>your</u> mark with this puzzle. There are seven men named Mark on the list below — three football players, two baseball players, one hockey player, and one basketball player. Can you find the Marks in the list? The symbol next to the athlete's name is his sport. When you find a last name to go with Mark, write the letter you find to the left of that last name in the "Scrambled Mark" space at the bottom of the page. After you've found all seven letters, unscramble them to find yet another famous Mark!

A. Dickerson 🏈   B. Pippen 🏀   C. Grace ⚾

D. Becker 🎾   E. Duper 🏈   F. Malone 🏀

G. Rypien 🏈   H. Gretzky 🏒   I. Langston ⚾

J. Clemens ⚾   K. Smith 🏈   L. Marino 🏈

M. Jackson 🏀   N. Thomas ⚾   O. Moon 🏈

P. Bowe 🥊   Q. Puckett ⚾   R. Messier 🏒

S. Fielder ⚾   T. O'Neal 🏀   U. Sandberg ⚾

V. Rice 🏈   W. Carrier 🏈   X. Belfour 🏒

Y. Gonzalez ⚾   Z. Wilkins 🏀

SCRAMBLED MARK:

— — — — — — —

UNSCRAMBLED MARK:

— — — — —

23

WORLD OF SPORTS WORD FIND

Here's a world of 17 sports for you to find, across and up and down in the word find puzzle on the opposite page. The first one is circled for you. Once you've found all the sports, go row by row in the word find (from left to right starting at the top) and write the leftover letters, in order, in the secret message spaces under the puzzle. Then you'll see the secret message!

THE SPORTS

BASEBALL   BASKETBALL   BOWLING

DIVING   FOOTBALL   GOLF

GYMNASTICS   HOCKEY   LACROSSE

RUGBY   SAILING   SKIING

SOCCER   SWIMMING   TENNIS

VOLLEYBALL   WRESTLING

```
V I G G Y M N A S T I C S
O T O S N L A C R O S S E
L O L T R U G B Y W H E D
L T F B A S E B A L L H I
E E H R Y S A I L I N G V
Y S O O U W I N O R L O I
B K C S F O O T B A L L N
A I K B O W L I N G E I G
L I E B A S K E T B A L L
L N Y T S H O W Y O U P L
A G Y S W I M M I N G T H
T E N N I S E S O C C E R
G A W R E S T L I N G M E
```

SECRET MESSAGE:

__ __ , __ __ __ __ __ __ __ __ __ __ __

__ __ __ __ __ __ __ __ __ __ __ __ __ __ ;

__ __ , __ __ __ __ __ __ __

__ __ __ __ __ __ __ __ __ __ __

25

SECRET SPORTS CODE

Be a sports detective! Decode the secret clue and answer by using the pictures of sports equipment instead of letters. Each piece of equipment — such as a ball, bat, or net — stands for a particular letter of the alphabet. Use the decoder key to crack the code and spell out the clue and the answer on the opposite page!

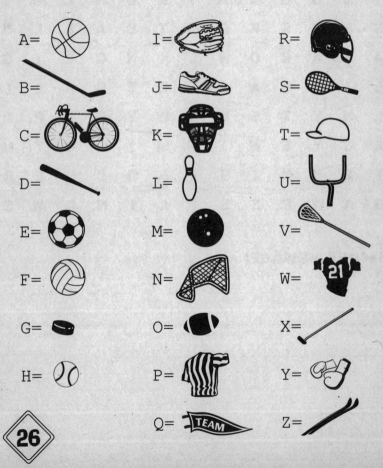

5 WORD CLUE:

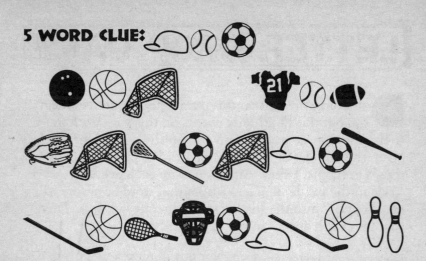

2 WORD ANSWER:

CLUE:

THE MANWHO
INVENTED
BASKETBALL

ANSWER:

___ ___ ___ ___ ___ ___ ___

___ ___ ___ ___ ___ ___ ___ ___

LETTER DROP GAME

Don't drop the ball on this puzzle, just the letters! Can you put the 15 athletic events on this page each in their proper space in the word grid on the next page? You are given the number of letters in the word or phrase in parentheses in the list below. After you write each event in its space in the puzzle, one letter from that word or phrase will be "dropped" into the shaded space directly below it. Then that letter will appear in the next word or phrase.

Let's start with the word SOCCER. Under SOCCER are spaces for a seven-letter word. But one of the spaces is shaded. That means the letter in that shaded space is exactly the same as the letter directly above it — in this case, it's an "S." Find the only seven-letter event with an "S" as the first letter, and go on from there. We've filled POLE VAULT also, and the "O" in POLE will drop down into the next word. Remember, the shaded box means that letter is **exactly** the same as the one above it. When you're done, write the letters from the shaded boxes in order in the spaces at the bottom of the next page and spell out where all of these events can be found!

THE EVENTS:

VOLLEYBALL (10)	SWIMMING (8)
HAMMER THROW (11)	UNEVEN BARS (10)
FIELD HOCKEY (11)	BASKETBALL (10)
HIGH JUMP (8)	DISCUS THROW (11)
WRESTLING (9)	LONG JUMP (8)
SHOT PUT (7)	GYMNASTICS (10)
TRIPLE JUMP (10)	CYCLING (7)

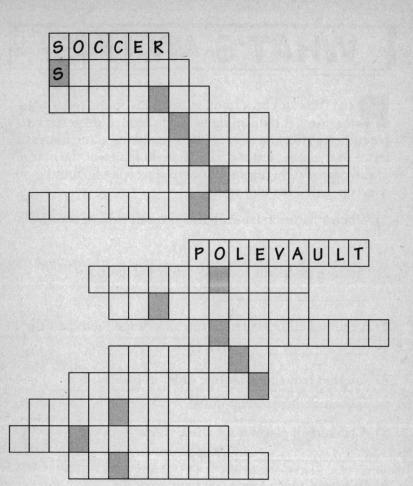

WHERE TO FIND THESE EVENTS:

___ ___ ___ ___ ___ ___

___ ___ ___ ___ ___ ___ ___ ___

WHAT'S MY LINE?

Read the clues below and write in the sports terms with the word "LINE" in them. Then look at the letters in parentheses after the answer blank and draw a line from one letter to the other letter in the group of letters at the bottom of the page. We've drawn 4 lines to start you off. You should wind up with a familiar word.

1) When a batter in baseball hits the ball hard, it is called a
_____ (B, C)

2) During a game, the football coach stands on the
_____ (F, I)

3) A tennis ball has been hit too far when it lands past the
_____ (H, I)

4) Another name for a batting order in baseball is a
_____ (J, M)

5) A basketball player takes a free throw from the
_____ (K, N)

6) To score a touchdown, you must cross the
_____ (L, O)

A   D   F   H   J   M

K   N

B   C   E   G   I   L   O

TWIN SEARCH

Gear up for this picture search puzzle! Two of the groups of sports gear below contain the same exact pieces of equipment, but in a different order. The other four groups are different from each other. Can you find the two groups that have the same pieces of sports equipment?

1.

2.

3.

4.

5.

6.

WHO, WHAT, WHERE, WHEN?

How much do you know about sports? Put your sports
brain to the test with these multiple choice questions!

WHO ♦ ♦ ♦

1. has the most career grand slams in the major leagues?
   - A. Babe Ruth
   - B. Hank Aaron
   - C. Lou Gehrig
   - D. Willie Mays

2. quarterbacked the San Francisco 49ers to four Super Bowl victories?
   - A. Joe Montana
   - B. John Elway
   - C. Steve Young
   - D. Terry Bradshaw

3. has the most career rushing yards in NFL history?
   - A. O.J. Simpson
   - B. Jim Brown
   - C. Earl Campbell
   - D. Walter Payton

4. was <u>not</u> a member of the Dream Team in the 1992 Summer Olympics?
   - A. Larry Bird
   - B. Karl Malone
   - C. Tim Hardaway
   - D. Scottie Pippen

WHAT ♦ ♦ ♦

1. was Kareem Abdul-Jabbar's original name?
   - A. Lew Alcindor
   - B. Bob Lanier
   - C. Cassius Clay
   - D. Bobby Moore

2. state has the most major league baseball teams?
   - A. Texas
   - B. California
   - C. New York
   - D. Illinois

3. was Babe Ruth's real first name?
   - A. George
   - B. Pete
   - C. Tyrus
   - D. Babe

4. team did Joe Namath lead to a Super Bowl victory?
   A. Colts   B. Giants   C. Packers   D. Jets

WHERE • • •

1. is the Football Hall of Fame located?
   A. Canton, Ohio   B. Cooperstown, NY
   C. Springfield, Mass.   D. Chicago, Ill.

2. did Shaquille O'Neal go to college?
   A. Virginia   B. Indiana
   C. Louisiana State   D. North Carolina

3. did the Dodgers play baseball before moving to Los Angeles?
   A. Boston   B. Brooklyn
   C. Milwaukee   D. Philadelphia

4. were the 1992 Summer Olympics?
   A. Barcelona, Spain   B. Los Angeles, Cal.
   C. Atlanta, Ga   D. Lake Placid, NY

WHEN • • •

1. did Jackie Robinson become the first black player in baseball?
   A. 1876   B. 1919   C. 1947   D. 1964

2. did the U.S. Olympic hockey team last win a gold medal?
   A. 1912   B. 1936   C. 1972   D. 1980

3. did the Chicago Bears win the Super Bowl?
   A. 1967   B. 1972   C. 1986   D. 1990   Never

4. did a terrible earthquake in San Francisco interrupt the World Series?
   A. 1907   B. 1965   C. 1983   D. 1989

33

WORD PLAY

Picture this! Each of these word pictures stands for a sports term. The trick is to read them in a different way. For example, the first one is another way of saying "hole-in-one" (a hole in the number one). The rest are up to you!

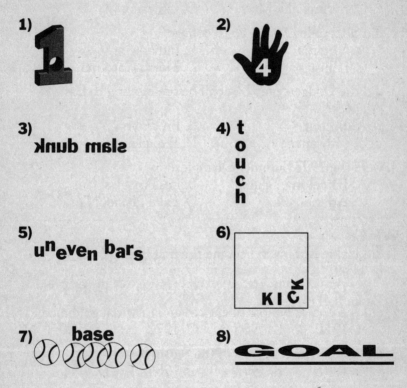

1)

2)

3) slam dunk

4) t
o
u
c
h

5) uneven bars

6) KICK

7) base

8) GOAL

THE NAME GAME

What happens when you combine the names of basketball players Michael Jordan and Rick Fox? You get Michael J. Fox! Or how about when you combine former baseball players Bert Campaneris and Ernie Banks? You get Bert and Ernie! Take a look at the athletes' names that are paired on each line, and see what you can make of them.

1. Baseball player **Dwight Gooden** and basketball player **Alonzo Mourning**

2. Hockey player **Mario Lemieux** and race car driver **Mario Andretti**

3. Former baseball stars **Mickey Mantle, Minnie Minoso, and Don Drysdale**

4. Baseball players **Rob Deer** and **Brian Hunter**

5. Former basketball star **Earvin "Magic" Johnson** and baseball star **Juan Gonzalez**

6. Basketball player **Hersey Hawkins** and football player **Matt Bahr**

7. Basketball coach **Doug Moe**, rightfielder **Larry Walker,** and Harlem Globetrotter **Curly Neal**

8. Former gymnast **Bart Connors** and football great **O.J. Simpson**

35

"T" IT UP

Below is a list of 25 of the greatest golfers in history. The last names of the golfers appear in the puzzle on the next page, but each name has a few letters missing. Can you fill in the names of all the golfers by filling in the missing letters? Get ready to " T " off!

GOLFERS:

Seve BALLESTEROS

Patty BERG

Nick FALDO

Walter HAGEN

Hale IRWIN

Tom KITE

Byron NELSON

Greg NORMAN

Gary PLAYER

Sam SNEAD

Lee TREVINO

Tom WATSON

Babe ZAHARIAS

Pat BRADLEY

Fred COUPLES

Raymond FLOYD

Ben HOGAN

Bobby JONES

Nancy LOPEZ

Jack NICKLAUS

Arnold PALMER

Gene SARAZEN

Curtis STRANGE

Harry VARDON

Mickey WRIGHT

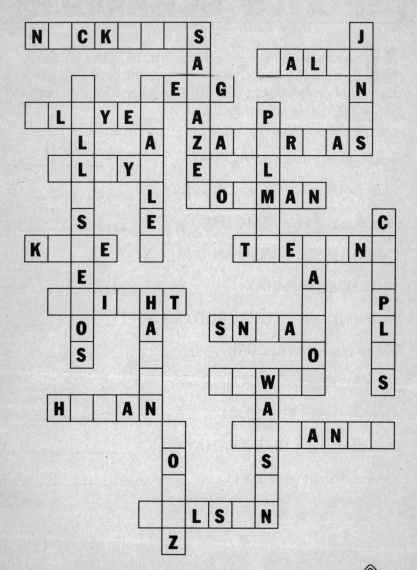

SPORTS SCRAMBLE

Unscramble each of the athletes' names. Then circle them in the word find on the opposite page written across and up and down. The first one is done for you, but the ball is in your court now!

Tennis player Jennifer **PACIRIAT** — CAPRIATI

Basketball forward Charles **KLERBAY** — *Barkley*

First baseman Frank **SMOTHA** — *Thomas*

Quarterback Joe **TONMAAN** — *Montana*

Pitcher Greg **DUMDAX** — *Maddux*

Basketball center Dikembe **BOOTMUM** — *Mutombo*

Tennis player Jim **RECURIO** — _____

Wide Receiver Jerry **ERIC** — *Rice*

Catcher Darren **TUDLOAN** — *Dolton*

Basketball guard Tim **DRAWHAYA** — *Hardaway*

Gymnast Shannon **RILMEL** — *Miler*

```
H I N O B Y M O N T A N A
D A U L T O N P S A Y B R
E N E A C D S A M M O Y H
Y T S U A R M I L L E R A
J H E M P E V S O E L I R
E O C O R N Z R E G S F D
C M K S I E X I O R M D A
O A Y M A R N C W N U I W
U S D Y T I C E K E T R A
R A F R I O L G E P O K Y
I M A D D U X C T B M N I
E R E V Y R E G E K B D R
R E B A R K L E Y T O F A
```

39

WORD WITHIN A WORD

Many sports words actually have other words inside them. For example, you can find the word "FOOT" in "FOOTBALL," and the word "IN" can be found in "SINGLE." Can you figure out the following eight sports words if you're only given the words inside them?

1. The wide receiver leaped to _c_ **A T** _c_ _h_ the pass in the end zone.

2. The hockey player who passes the puck to a goal scorer is credited with an _a_ _s_ **S I S** _t_.

3. It's a _s_ **W I N** _g_ and a miss. Strike one!

4. The person who calls the offensive plays in football is the _q_ _u_ **A R T** _e_ _r_ _b_ _a_ _c_ _k_

5. The **C E N T** _e_ _r_ is always the first football player to touch the ball.

6. Shaquille O'Neal likes to put the ball in the _b_ **A S K** _e_ _t_.

7. A shorter name for a three-base hit is a _t_ **R I P** _l_ _e_.

8. Bows and arrows can be found in the sport of _a_ _r_ _c_ **H E R** _y_.

DOUBLE PLAY

There are many well-known sports terms that are made up of two words, such as *slam dunk* or *goal line*. The following list of 20 words can be made into 10 two-word terms. Can you match up the right words together? The first one is done for you, but it's your job to pair off the rest!

~~BALANCE~~	BASE	~~BEAM~~
BOWLING	DOWN	WIDE
THROW	FREE	FIRST
GRAND	END	STOLEN
PIN	HOOK	RECEIVER
POLE	SLAM	ZONE
SHOT	VAULT	

BALANCE _BEAM_ _____ _____

_____ _____ _____ _____

_____ _____ _____ _____

_____ _____ _____ _____

_____ _____ _____ _____

RE +

Each of the five collections of pictures below represents the name of an athlete. To sound out their names, add or subtract as directed. The symbol to the left of the rebus is the athlete's sport. Print the names in the spaces under each rebus. Then copy the shaded letters into the spaces at the end of the puzzle. These letters spell out the first name of the legendary athlete whose last name is

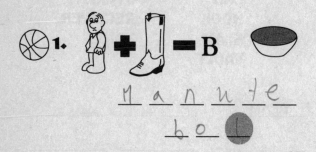

1.

M a n u t e
b o l

2.

B O
J a c k s o n

3. <u>H e ⬤ sh e ll</u>
<u>w a l k e r</u>

4. 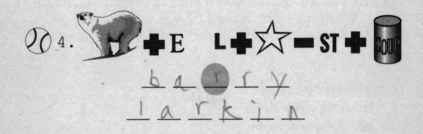 +E   L+☆ –ST + SOUP

<u>b a ⬤ r r y</u>
<u>l a r k i n</u>

5.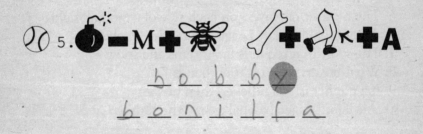

<u>b o b b ⬤ y</u>
<u>b o n i l l a</u>

ATHLETE'S FIRST NAME: <u>L a r r y</u>

WORD SPIRAL

We've come around the bases to another word spiral! Fill in the spiral puzzle on the next page in a clockwise direction (↷), using the clues on this page. The last letter of each word will be the first letter of the next word. Each word ends at the square where you see the next number. Answers 1 and 2 have been filled in to show you how it works. When the puzzle is finished, you will find a secret nine-letter name down the shaded middle column on the grid!

1. Riddick Bowe's sport
2. Tennis superstar Steffi _____ **GRAF**
3. The opposite of slow
4. A field goal is worth _____ points.
5. The number of players on each side of a football field
6. A National Hockey League team: the Quebec _____
7. The sport that requires mountains and snow
8. What boxers wear on their hands
9. If a pitcher isn't a reliever, then he's a _____.
10. A Major League baseball team: the Kansas City _____
11. Someone who can hit from both sides of the plate is a _____-hitter.
12. Two quarters in a football game make up one _____.
13. If there's a penalty, a referee throws a yellow _____.
14. Seattle Mariners slugger Ken _____, Jr.
15. This Milwaukee Brewers star reached 3,000 hits: Robin

16. Baseball Hall of Famer Tom Seaver's initials
17. A short word for statistic
18. The shortstop tries to _____ the person stealing second base (rhymes with bag).
19. The color worn by the Boston Celtics and the Philadelphia Eagles

¹B	O	X	I	N	²G	R	A	³F
	⁸6	1	o	o	e	⁹s	A	
	13			14		t	S	
12	17			18		a	⁴T	
7	16					r	h	
			19			t	r	
		15				e	e	
11					¹⁰r	⁵e		
		6						

SECRET NAME:

___ ___ ___ ___   ___ ___ ___ ___

45

IN THE NICK(NAME) OF TIME

By now your nickname could be Puzzlemeister. But can you match these athletes with **their** nicknames? Write the athletes' real name in the spaces to the right of each nickname. Then write the shaded letters in order at the bottom of the page to see baseball great Lou Gehrig's nickname.

THE ATHLETES:

Charles Barkley	Roger Clemens	Wayne Gretzky
Dwight Gooden	Karl Malone	Michael Jordan
David Robinson	Andre Dawson	Deion Sanders
Earvin Johnson	Lawrence Taylor	

1. "LT" _ _ _ _ _ _ _ _ _ _ _ _ _ _

2. "Dr. K" _ _ _ _ _ _ _ _ _ _ _ _

3. "The Admiral" _ _ _ _ _ _ _ _ _ _ _ _ _

4. "Sir Charles" _ _ _ _ _ _ _ _ _ _ _ _ _

5. "Prime Time" _ _ _ _ _ _ _ _ _ _ _ _

6. "The Hawk" _ _ _ _ _ _ _ _ _ _ _

7. "Magic" _ _ _ _ _ _ _ _ _ _ _ _ _

8. "Air" _ _ _ _ _ _ _ _ _ _ _ _

9. "The Mailman" _ _ _ _ _ _ _ _ _ _

10. "Rocket" _ _ _ _ _ _ _ _ _ _ _ _ _

11. "The Great One" _ _ _ _ _ _ _ _ _ _ _ _

Lou Gehrig's nickname:

_ _ _   _ _ _ _ _

PENNANT RACE

Joe Boxer was knocked out in the third round of his fight with Kid Glove. When he came to, Joe Boxer saw the pennants in the sports arena as they appear below. The first three letters of one sport were mixed up with the last three letters of another sport on each of the six pennants. For each pennant, can you find the right three letters so that you can read one sport on each pennant?

SOCING

HOCING

BOXKEY

DIVCER

SKINIS

TENING

SPORT #1: _____

SPORT #2: _____

SPORT #3: _____

SPORT #4: _____

SPORT #5: _____

SPORT #6: _____

47

COURTSIDE CROSSWORD

Take a shot at these basketball clues and see how much you know about the NBA. The first answer is "down" for you.

ACROSS

1. The object of the game is to put the ball in the _____.
4. The basketball team in Indiana
6. David Robinson's position
7. The abbreviation for National Basketball Association
9. The basketball team in Miami
10. A bank shot from under the basket is called a lay__.
11. A good pass that leads to a basket is called an _____.
13. Tim Hardaway's position
16. You can't walk with the ball; you have to _____ it.
17. The game starts with the opening ____.
19. If fouled while taking a shot, you can ___ two free throws.
23. When two players have the ball at the same time, it's a ____ ball.
24. New York Knicks center Patrick _____.
25. Karl Malone's nickname

DOWN

1. A bank shot bounces off the **BACKBOARD**.
2. The basketball team in Phoenix
3. A shot from 25 feet away is worth _____ points
4. Each foul shot is worth one _____.
5. The term for grabbing the ball after a missed basket
8. The NBA players who won the gold in the Olympics

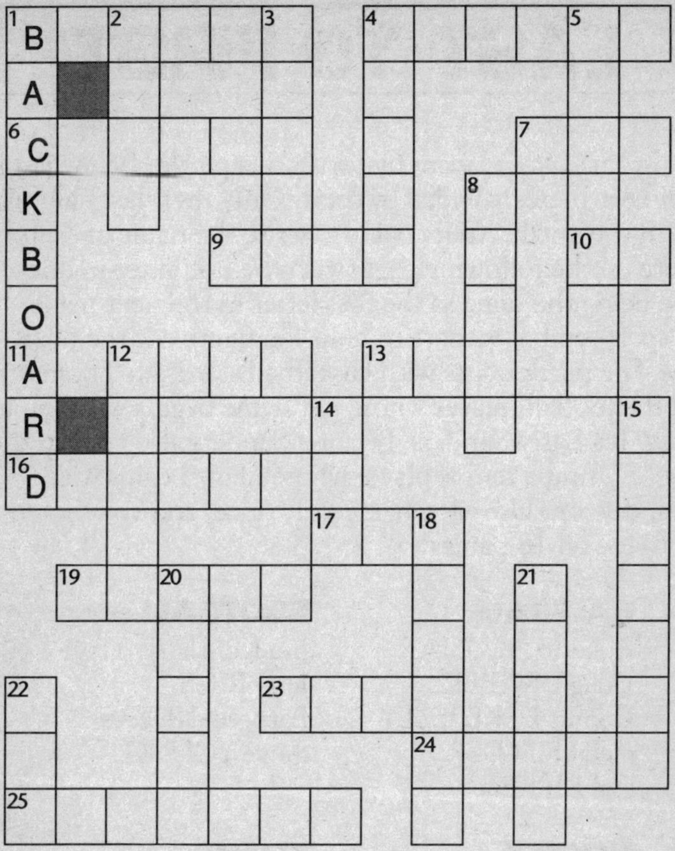

were called the ________ team.

12. A basket that goes in without even touching the rim.
14. The ______ is attached to the underside of the hoop.
15. The team that scores the most points is the ______ team.
18. Chicago Bulls superstar Scottie ______
20. Orlando Magic center Shaquille ______
21. Earvin Johnson's nickname
22. A free throw shot that's too short will bounce off the __.

LAST TO FIRST

Can you go from last to first with this puzzle? Below is a list of 18 athletes, divided by sport. Only their last names are used in the puzzle. Your goal is to write the name of each athlete on the following page, with the last letter in one name being the same as the first letter in the next name. The sport symbol is there to help you figure out the next name. The puzzle starts with basketball star Isiah Thomas. Find the football player whose last name begins with the letter "S." It's Barry Sanders. Because Sanders also ends in the letter "S", find a tennis player whose name begins with "S"–and so on. Use each name only once, and you should be able to use all 18 names!

BASEBALL
Roberto ALOMAR
Doug DRABEK
Dennis ECKERSLEY
Cecil FIELDER
Cal RIPKEN

FOOTBALL
Jim KELLY
Jerry RICE
Barry ~~SANDERS~~
Steve YOUNG

HOCKEY
Brett HULL
Steve LARMER
Steve YZERMAN

TENNIS
Steffi GRAF
Martina NAVRATILOVA
Michael STICH

BASKETBALL
Larry NANCE
Mitch RICHMOND
Isiah ~~THOMAS~~

50

1. 🏀 THOMAS

2. 🏈 SANDERS

3. 🎾 _____

4. 🏒 _____

5. 🏒 _____

6. 🎾 _____

7. 🎾 _____

8. 🎾 _____

9. 🏈 _____

10. 🎾 _____

11. 🏈 _____

12. 🎾 _____

13. 🎾 _____

14. 🏀 _____

15. 🎾 _____

16. 🏈 _____

17. 🏒 _____

18. 🏀 _____

DOUBLE JEOPARDY #2

Let's play two! On the left is a symbol of the athlete's sport, and on the right is a scrambled name. Unscramble the names and write them in the spaces on the right. Then write the letters from the shaded boxes in each word, in order, in the secret phrase spaces below the puzzle. When you've finished, you'll see a familiar sports phrase.

1. TEVSE UNGYO ___ ___ ___ ___ ___ ___ ___ ___ ___ ___

2. RIDRACH ___ ___ ___ ___ ___ ___ ___
   TEPTY ___ ___ ___ ___ ___

3. NIVKE ___ ___ ___ ___ ___
   SHOONJN ___ ___ ___ ___ ___ ___ ___

4. BROIN NUTOY ___ ___ ___ ___ ___ ___ ___ ___ ___ ___

5. TOSCTIE ___ ___ ___ ___ ___ ___ ___
   PENPIP ___ ___ ___ ___ ___ ___

6. RAYG ___ ___ ___ ___
   DIFFELSHE ___ ___ ___ ___ ___ ___ ___ ___ ___

7. HIPL MISMS ___ ___ ___ ___ ___ ___ ___ ___ ___

8. VONDE ITEWH ___ ___ ___ ___ ___ ___ ___ ___ ___

SECRET PHRASE:

___ ___ ___ ___ ___ ___ ___ ___ ___ ___

___ ___ ___ ___ ___ ___ ___

STRANGE SEVENTH INNING STRETCH

Sing "Take Me Out to the Ballgame" like you've never sung it before! Two people can play, one person will be the Reader. It's the Reader's job to ask the other player for words and to fill in the blanks. The WORD KEY below has examples of the kinds of words that are needed. When the Reader has filled in all the blanks, he or she should read the finished story out loud. It may sound crazy, but that's what makes the game so much fun!

WORD KEY:

    noun examples: classroom, doorknob, movie, pig
    verb examples: run, laugh, urge, dribble
    adjective — a word that describes a person, place or thing
    adjective examples: green, enormous, smart, happy
    number examples: 5, 16, 142
    plural — add an "s" to the end

Take me out to the _____, take me out to the

_____. _____ me some _____ and
  (NOUN)   (VERB)   (NOUN)

_____. I don't care if I ever get _____
  (NOUN)   (ADJECTIVE)

For it's _____, _____, _____ for
  (VERB)   (SAME VERB)   (SAME VERB)

the home team. If they don't _____ it's a shame.
                          (VERB)

For it's _____, _____, _____ _____
  (NUMBER)   (NUMBER)   (NUMBER)   (PLURAL NOUN)

you're _____ at the _____ _____!
  (ADJECTIVE)   (ADJECTIVE)   (NOUN)

SHARED LETTER QUIZ

The four sport words, phrases or names in each group below have only one letter in common. In group #1, the only letter that appears in every word is the letter P, which is written in the shared letter space and in the #1 space in the secret phrase. Find the letter that each of the other groups of words, phrases, or names have in common and write it in the space below the group and in its numbered space in the secret phrase When you are done, the secret phrase should spell out the most important word in sports.

1. FOOTBALL TERMS:
CLIPPING
DRAW PLAY
SCREEN PASS
PENALTY FLAG

shared letter: __P__

2. HALL OF FAMERS:
BABE RUTH
LOU GEHRIG
HANK AARON
JOHNNY BENCH

shared letter: ____

3. NBA TEAMS:
PISTONS
MAGIC
CAVALIERS
TIMBERWOLVES

shared letter: ____

4. SPORTS MOVIES:
THE NATURAL
FAST BREAK
BULL DURHAM
SLAPSHOT

shared letter: ____

5. BASEBALL STARS:
BONDS
SHEFFIELD
DAWSON
VAN SLYKE

shared letter: ____

6. FOOTBALL POSITIONS:
QUARTERBACK
LINEBACKER
GUARD
CENTER

shared letter: ____

54

7. NBA STARS:
JORDAN
ROBINSON
O'NEAL
LAETTNER

shared letter: ____

8. SPORTS EQUIPMENT:
HOCKEY PUCK
BASKETBALL HOOP
PITCHING RUBBER
GOAL POST

shared letter: ____

9. TENNIS STARS:
JIMMY CONNORS
ANDRE AGASSI
PETE SAMPRAS
STEFAN EDBERG

shared letter: ____

10. OLYMPIC EVENTS:
MARATHON
HIGH JUMP
SWIMMING
GYMNASTICS

shared letter: ____

11. NHL TEAMS:
NORTH STARS
SENATORS
JETS
LIGHTNING

shared letter: ____

12. GREAT RUNNING BACKS:
O.J. SIMPSON
TONY DORSETT
FRANCO HARRIS
GALE SAYERS

shared letter: ____

13. BASEBALL TERMS:
HOME RUN
SHUTOUT
STOLEN BASE
DOUBLE PLAY

shared letter: ____

SECRET WORD:

___	P	___	___	___	___	___	___	___	___	___	___	___
9	1	13	6	11	5	10	4	7	12	2	3	8

ANSWERS

PAGE 4-5, TWO-SPORT QUIZ
1. Drive (D), 2. Steal (E), 3. Pitch (I), 4. Shot (O), 5. Pin (N), 6. Slam (S), 7. Flag (A), 8. Run (N), 9. Guard (D), 10. Hike (E), 11. Strike (R), 12. Assist (S), Two-sport star: Deion Sanders

PAGE 6-7, WORD SPIRAL
1. Swing, 2. Goalpost, 3. Tee, 4. End zone, 5. Empty, 6. Young, 7. Gloves, 8. Star, 9. Raiders, 10. String, 11. Gain, 12. Nets, 13. Short, 14. Teammate, 15. Evel, 16. Loss, 17. Sub, 18. Bunt, 19. Toss, 20. Sand
Center phrase: Grand Slam

S	W	I	N	G	O	A	L	P
E	S	T	A	R	A	I	D	O
V	R	T	E	A	M	M	E	S
O	O	B	U	N	T	A	R	T
L	H	U	N	D	O	T	S	E
G	S	A	S	S	E	T	E	
N	T	S	O	L	E	V	R	N
U	E	N	I	A	G	N	I	D
O	Y	T	P	M	E	N	O	Z

PAGE 8, DOUBLE JEOPARDY #1
1. Matt Williams (AT), 2. Larry Johnson (LA), 3. Robin Ventura (NT), 4. Steffi Graf (AF), 5. Karl Malone (AL), 6. Scottie Pippen (CO), 7. Roger Clemens (NS)
Secret team: Atlanta Falcons

PAGE 9, SPORTS SCATTERGRAM
The one piece of equipment not repeated is HELMET.

PAGE 10-11, SAME NAME GAME
1. Michael, 2. Andre, 3. Chris, 4. Terry, 5. John, 6. Charles. 7. Barry, 8. Jim, 9. Steve, 10. Tom, 11. Dennis, 12. Jack, 13. Joe, 14. Tim, 15. Paul, 16. Fred

PAGE 12-13, ➡ GRIDIRON CROSSWORD

ANSWERS

PAGE 14-15, BOWLING FOR LETTERS

10-letter words or phrases:

1) gymnastics
2) basketball
3) linebacker
4) golf course
5) volleyball
6) goal tender
7) double play
8) backstroke

Other possible words:

staying, masts, stain, tin
skate, label, steak, base
black, break, lack, lean
flour, frogs, recluse, cool
label, valley, yell, love
trend, great, glared, teen
blade, plead, bold, boy
stack, track, coaster, break

PAGE 16, A,B, SIERRA

A–Tim Hardaway, B–Kirby Puckett, C–Andre Agassi, D–Dee Brown,
G–Reggie White, J–Jay Schroeder, L–John Elway, M–Emmitt Smith,
O–Dan Marino, T–Jennifer Capriati, U–Patrick Ewing, V–Davey
Allison, X–Clyde Drexler, Y–Mark McGwire, Z–Ozzie Smith

PAGE 17, TWO TIMES TWO

1. Warren Moon, 2. Brett Hull,
3. Emmitt Smith, 4. Bobby
Bonilla, 5. Scottie Pippen,
6. Randall Cunningham,
7. Darryl Strawberry
Triple Double: Oscar Robertson

PAGE 18-19, ➡
FOOTBALL FILL-IN

PAGE 20-21, RHYME TIME

1. clock, lock, rock, sock, block,
shock

2. sun, gun, done, run, fun, won

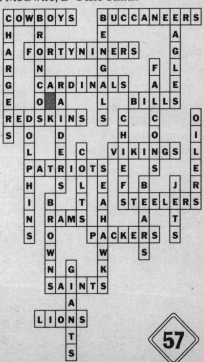

57

ANSWERS

PAGE 22,
THE SUM-MER GAME
1. 11, 2. 4, 3. 5, 4. 8, 5. 2,
6. 12, 7. 9, 8. 6, 9. 3.
The magic number is 44

PAGE 23, ON THE MARK
Scrambled Mark: CEGIM-RW
Unscrambled Mark: MCGWIRE

PAGE 24-25, WORLD OF
SPORTS WORD FIND ➡
Secret phrase: It's not whether you win or lose; It's how you play the game.

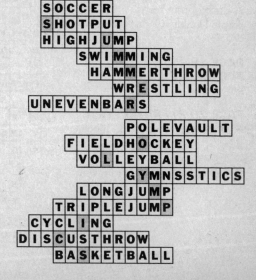

PAGE 26-27, SECRET SPORTS CODE
Clue: The man who invented basketball. **Answer:** James Naismith

PAGE 28-29, ➡
LETTER DROP GAME
Where to find these events: Summer Olympics

PAGE 30,
WHAT'S MY LINE?
1. line drive, 2. sideline,
3. baseline, 4. lineup,
5. foul line,
6. goal line.

58

ANSWERS

PAGE 31, TWIN SEARCH
#4 and #6 are the same

PAGE 32-33, WHO, WHAT, WHERE, WHEN?
WHO: 1. C, 2. A, 3. D, 4. C, WHAT: 1. A, 2. B, 3. A, 4. D,
WHERE: 1. A, 2. C, 3. B, 4. A, WHEN: 1. C, 2. D, 3. C, 4. D.

PAGE 34, WORD PLAY,
1. Hole-in-one, 2. forehand, 3. reverse slam dunk, 4. touchdown,
5. uneven bars, 6. corner kick, 7. base on balls, 8. goal line.

PAGE 35, THE NAME GAME
1. Gooden Mourning (Good Morning), 2. Mario Brothers, 3. Mickey,
Minnie and Donald, 4 Deer Hunter, 5. Magic Juan (Magic Wand),
6. Hersey Bahr (Hershey Bar), 7. Moe, Larry and Curly, 8. Bart Simpson

PAGE 36-37, ➡ "T" IT UP

PAGE 38-39, ➡
SPORTS SCRAMBLE
1. Capriati, 2. Barkley,
3. Thomas, 4. Montana,
5. Maddux, 6. Mutombo,
7. Courier, 8. Rice,
9. Daulton, 10. Hardaway,
11. Miller

PAGE 40,
WORD WITHIN A WORD
1. catch, 2. assist, 3. swing,
4. quarterback, 5. center,
6. basket, 7. triple, 8.
archery.

```
H  I  N  O  B  Y (M  O  N  T  A  N  A)
(D  A  U  L  T  O  N) P  S  A  Y  B  R
E  N  E  A (C  D  S  A  M  M  O  Y  H
Y (T  S  U  A  R (M  I  L  L  E  R) A
J  H  E  M  P  E  V  S  O  R  L  I  R
E  O  C  O  R  N  Z (R  E  G  S  F  D
C  M  K  S  I  E  X  I  O  R (M  D  A
O  A  Y  M  A  R  N  C  W  N  U  I  W
U  S  D  Y  T  I  C  E  K  E  T  R  A
R  A  F  R  I  O  L  G  E  P  O  K  Y
I (M  A  D  D  U  X) C  T  B  M  N  I
E  R  E  V  Y  R  E  G  E  K  B  D  R
R  E (B  A  R  K  L  E  Y) T (O  F  A
```

PAGE 41, DOUBLE PLAY
1. Balance Beam, 2. Bowling Pin, 3. End Zone, 4. Free Throw, 5. First
Down, 6. Grand Slam, 7. Hook Shot, 8. Pole Vault, 9. Stolen Base,
10. Wide Receiver

PAGE 42-43, RE +
1. Manute Bol, 2. Bo Jackson, 3. Herschel Walker, 4. Barry Larkin,
5. Bobby Bonilla
Athlete's first name: Larry (Bird)

PAGE 44-45, WORD SPIRAL ➡
1. Boxing, 2. Graf, 3. Fast, 4. Three, 5. Eleven,
6. Nordiques, 7. Skiing, 8. Gloves, 9. Starter,
10. Royals, 11. Switch, 12. Half, 13. Flag,
14. Griffey, 15. Yount, 16. TS, 17. Stat,
18. Tag, 19. Green
Secret name: Nolan Ryan

B	O	X	I	N	G	R	A	F
I	N	G	L	O	V	E	S	A
I	A	L	F	L	A	G	T	S
K	H	S	T	A	T	R	A	T
S	C	T	E	N	A	I	R	H
E	T	N	E	R	G	F	T	R
U	I	U	O	Y	E	F	E	E
Q	W	S	L	A	Y	O	R	E
I	D	R	O	N	E	V	E	L

ANSWERS

PAGE 46, IN THE NICK(NAME) OF TIME
1. Lawrence Taylor, 2. Dwight Gooden, 3. David Robinson, 4. Charles Barkley, 5. Deion Sanders, 6. Andre Dawson, 7. Earvin Johnson, 8. Michael Jordan, 9. Karl Malone, 10. Roger Clemens 11. Wayne Gretzky
Lou Gehrig's nickname: The Iron Horse

PAGE 47, PENNANT RACE
Six sports: Soccer, Boxing, Skiing, Hockey, Diving, Tennis

PAGE 48-49, ➡ COURTSIDE CROSSWORD

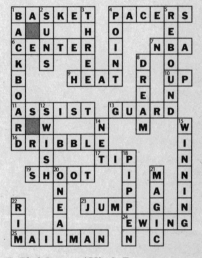

PAGE 50-51, LAST TO FIRST
1. Thomas, 2. Sanders, 3. Stich, 4. Hull, 5. Larmer, 6. Ripken, 7. Navratilova, 8. Alomar, 9. Rice, 10. Eckersley, 11. Young, 12. Graf, 13. Fielder, 14. Richmond, 15. Drabek, 16. Kelly, 17. Yzerman, 18. Nance

PAGE 52, DOUBLE JEOPARDY #2
1. Steve Young (ST), 2. Richard Petty (RI), 3. Kevin Johnson (KE), 4. Robin Yount (OU), 5. Scottie Pippen (TT), 6. Gary Sheffield (HE), 7. Phil Simms (SI), 8. Devon White(DE.
Secret Phrase: Strike out the side

PAGE 53, STRANGE SEVENTH INNING STRETCH
The answers are what ever you want them to be!

PAGE 54-55, SHARED LETTER QUIZ
1. P, 2. H, 3. I, 4. A, 5. S, 6. R, 7. N, 8. P, 9. S, 10. M, 11. T, 12. S, 13. O
Secret word: Sportsmanship